MW00789931

Lebanese Arabic Phrasebook Vol. 2

HIBA NAJEM

Writers: Hiba Najem & Naim El Hajj
Copywriter: Lynn Najem
Cover Design: Fouad Rizk

LearnLebaneseArabic@gmail.com
Lebanese-Arabic.com

DEDICATION

While living in Beirut, I have had the chance to meet a lot of foreigners who visit the country each for their own purpose. Many of them were struggling with the language, since the Fusha, which they had made a lot effort learning, didn't seem to help, despite being an extremely eloquent modern standard language that unites all Arabic speaking countries. The reason for that struggle is that every Arab country has its own dialect that differs from Fusha.

If your destination is Lebanon, then I recommend this book that will provide you enough confidence and skills to converse with locals. I dedicate my book to my language and to everyone who is willing to learn it, and above all to the love of my country, a peculiar love, I must admit, for a place that is hard to live in but also harder to leave.

CONTENTS

PREFACE

So yes, I'm still here in Beirut, Lebanon asking myself everyday whether I should stay or leave in this corrupt country where we often find ourselves struggling to find a bit of happiness and something close to peace. Beirut is getting even more crowded, and to think that we never thought it possible! From poor public transportation, to lack of green spaces and of course the never-ending waste crisis that sadly no authority is trying to solve, one would wonder what makes so many remain here.

Putting aside all of the above, there still are some very convincing reasons to stay! I simply cannot imagine my days passing without seeing my family, friends, my wonderfully moderate summer-like winter, my happy hours in Badaro or Gemayze, or my road trips to our beautiful villages. With all the new positive vibes growing stronger, I still have high hopes in Lebanon, I believe in change, in the new generation that is willing to create, read, plant, or even recycle in the hope of creating more sustainable living conditions in this nation that is yet to model its true identity.

Having said this, I really want to thank you for following me on my YouTube channel that is celebrating its sixth year by now. Thank you for believing in a better Lebanon just like me. Thank you for coming back, for visiting, for finding your Lebanese roots, for teaching your children and also grand children your original dialect, thank you for your curiosity in a culture that you've grown up in or just heard about.

Thus, I dedicate this second book to all the good reasons that make me happy to stay here.

Wishing for peace and peace only, salam

سلام

INTRODUCTION

The following introduction is also present in the previous volume. It mainly lays out the method and guidelines that will be used throughout the book. If you already own Vol. 1 you probably have read this and already understand how it works. If not, I recommend you go through it because it will make reading the translations and transliterations much easier.

The method of teaching is vaguely inspired by the Rosetta Stone method that teaches the dialect through using practical sentences instead of memorizing strict grammatical rules.

All the words and phrases are transcribed from the videos, so there will be a reference to the relevant video below each sentence. You will be able to hear the correct pronunciation in order to master your accent and find detailed explanations of each word in complex phrases.

The sentences will be divided into themes like "Introductions" or "Traveling" and they will be written in 3 forms:

1.   In English first.
2.   Then in Lebanese transliteration (Latin alphabet) for people

who can't read Arabic.

3.   And eventually in Lebanese (Arabic alphabet) for those who are Arabic literate.

Transliteration Guidelines

Since the Arabic alphabet is quite different from the Latin one that does not include the same letters, we'll have to agree upon certain rules that we'll use throughout the book as to avoid any confusion. The chosen representations will be based on their simplicity in contrast with the academic but more complex symbols such as [ʔ] or (ḥ). There will be a table presenting each letter and its transliterated representation, preceded by an explanation of some of the letters used. While the table might only be useful for Arabic readers, the explanation will help all readers to recognize the sounds of the transliteration. If any of the following information seems too complicated for you, don't worry, you will find it to be simpler as you go along and read the actual words and phrases. These are just guidelines you can refer to if you find any difficulty in reading transliterations:

1.   The Hamza (ء) which is a glottal stop, is not a full letter and is not one of the 28 letters of the alphabet but it is widely used in the language and especially in the Lebanese dialect, as in most Lebanese areas, the Qaf (ق) (pronounced as a "K" or a "Q" in standard Arabic) is pronounced as a Hamza and labeled as a glottal stop. The Hamza is phonetically represented as /ʔ/ while academically represented as a "modifier letter right half ring" (ʾ) which will be replaced by an apostrophe in this book ('). You might find it to be represented with the number (2) on the web, as this is the conventional chatting representation of it, inspired by the inverted similarity in shape of the (2) and the (ء).

2.   The Aleph (ا), the first letter of the Arabic alphabet, takes many forms, depending on its accentuation and on the placement of the Hamza in relation to it, facts that change the way it sounds. It might sound as a glottal stop or as a long vowel. For this reason, in cases where it sounds as a glottal stop it will be transliterated as a simple Hamza (') and in cases where it sounds like a vowel, it will be represented with the respective vowels (a), (e), (i), (o), or (ei). The last, (ei), is used as the sound of the accentuated letter (é).

3

3. Thaa' (ث), is an Arabic letter that sounds like (th) in English words like (th)ink or ba(th), but in the Lebanese dialect it is most commonly replaced by either a (t) or an (s) sound. So it might be written in words as a (ث), but pronounced as is written in the Transliteration. (Ex: Snow=Talej= ثلج)

4. The Arabic letter (ع) or Ayn has no similar letters or sounds in the Latin alphabet. It is articulated with the back of the throat and the root of the tongue. It is phonetically represented as /ʕ/, while its academic representation is the "modifier letter left half ring" (ʿ) which is similar to the representation of the Hamza. In order to avoid any confusion between the Hamza and the Ayn, the latter will be represented as it is in chatting forums with the number (3) because of its mirrored resemblance to (ع), letter "3ayn".

5. Ghayn (غ) is a variant of 3ayn (ع) in shape but is different in sound. The closest popular equivalent to its sound is the Parisian French (r). It is phonetically represented as /ɣ/ but most commonly transliterated as (gh) which we will use throughout the book.

6. The Haa' (ح) which is similar to the 3ayn in articulation (with the back of the throat and the root of the tongue) but different in phonation is represented phonetically as /ħ/ and academically as (ħ) while in this book it will be represented as a capital (H) which is usually the simplest symbol of the Haa'. You might find that it is sometimes written as a (7) because of the number's resemblance to the upper part of (ح).

7. The Khaa' (خ) is pronounced in a way that is very similar to German, Scottish, and Polish (ch), Russian (x), and Spanish (j). It is phonetically represented as /x/, while its most common transliteration is (kh) which is used almost everywhere and is therefore used in this book. You might also find it to be represented as (5) which also resembles a distorted mirrored (خ) missing the dot.

8. Thaal (ذ) and Thahh (ظ) which are variants of each other, and resemble the sound of the English (th) in (th)is or fea(th)er, are most commonly replaced by either a (d) or a (z). Ex: Memory=-Zeikra= ذاكرة)

9.   Finally, some words end with the sound (é), or might have this sound in the middle of the word. These will be transliterated as (eh) in the end, and (ei) in the middle.

As for the Lebanese words written in the Arabic alphabet, those ending with the (a) sound in Lebanese will be written:

1.   as (ا) whenever the same word in Modern Standard Arabic end with (ء) or (ا) like حَمراء or عَندها, written as حَمرا or عَندا

2.   as (ة) whenever the word is feminine and has a masculine version, like رايحة

3.   otherwise, they will be seen as (ـه)

The Arabic Letters and Their Transliteration According To the Lebanese Dialect

ا	a | i | o | e | ei
ب	b
ت	t
ث	t | s
ج	j
ح	H
خ	kh
د	d
ذ	d | z
ر	r
ز	z
س	s
ش	sh
ص	s
ض	d
ط	t
ظ	d | z
ع	3
غ	gh
ف	f

ق	ʼ
ك	k
ل	l
م	m
ن	n
ه	h
و	w | ou
ي	i | y

CHAPTER 1: BASIC LANGUAGE

Basic: the word basic means "aseis" in Lebanese. It could be used to say we are in the first stage of building the house, we are building the aseis.

An additional meaning would be "it wasn't meant to be in the first place": bil aseis (or aseisan), ma kenit zabta

Aseiseh on the other hand can be used to ask: is it something really important? Houwe chi hal'ad aseiseh?

Songs: kifak enta, Feyrouz (wait till she says enta el asasi/ aseiseh w bHebbak bil asas/aseis)

CLOCK

Time	wa'et
	وَقت

Timing	touw'eet
	توقيت
Hour	sei3a
	ساعَة
2 hours	se3tein
	ساعتين
Hours	se3at
	ساعات
Minute	d'i'a
	دقيقَة
2 minutes	d'i'tein
	دقيقتين
Minutes	da'eyi'
	دَقايق
Second	seinyeh
	ثانية
2 seconds	senitein
	ثانتين

Seconds	saweineh ثواني
A.M	abel el doher قَبل الضُهر
P.M	ba3ed el doher بَعد الضُهر
It's late	m'akhar مأخَر
It's early	bakkeer بكّير
What time is it?	addeh el sei3a? أدّي الساعَة؟
10 to 1	weHdeh 'ella 3ashra وحدة إلاّ عَشرَة
5 past 6	setteh w khamseh ستّة و خَمسة
5 to 6	setteh 'ella khamseh ستّة إلاّ خَمسة

11:45	tna3sh 'ella rebe3
	تنعش و ربع
2:30	tnein(tentein) w noss
	تنين (تنتين) و نُصّ
3:25	tleiteh w noss 'ella kham-seh
	تلاتي و نُصّ إلّأ خَمسة
3:35	tleiteh w noss w khamseh
	تلاتي و نُصّ و خَمسة
3:15	tleiteh w rebe3
	تلاتي و ربع
3:20	tleiteh w telet
	تلاتي و تلت
3:40	arb3a 'ella telet
	أربعة إلّأ تلت
I'll be there in an hour or two	raH ousal ba3ed sei3a aw se3tein
	رَح أوصَل بَعد ساعَة أو ساعتَين

I waited for you for half an hour	natartak/ natartik noss sei3a
	نَطَرتَك/ نَطَرتِك نُصّ ساعَة
My sister arrives in 3 hours	ekhteh wasleh (raH tousal) ba3ed tleit se3at
	إختي واصلي (رَح توصَل) بَعد تلات ساعات
I will be with you in a minute	d'i'a w bkoun ma3ak/ ma3ik
	دقيقَة و بكون مَعَك
What time is it Canada time?	addeh el sei3a bi touw'eet canada?
	اذَي الساعَة بتوقيت كَندا؟
I have a meeting tomorrow at 5 pm	3andeh ejtimei3/ maw3ad boukra 3al sei3a khamseh ba3ed el doher
	عَندي إجتماع/ مَوعَد بُكرا على ساعَة خَمسة بَعد الضُهر

INTERROGATIVE WORDS

Why?	leh/lesh? ليه/ ليش
When?	eimtan? أمتَن
Who?	meen? مين
Whose?	la meen? لَمين
How?	keef? كيف
What?	shou? شو
Where?	wein? وَين
What for?	la shou? لَشو

Since when?	min eimtan? مِن أمتَن
Why not?	lesh la'/ leh la'? ليش لاء
What else?	shou kamein? شو كَمان
How come?	keef ta? كيف تَ
How much?	addeh? أدّي
Why are you angry?	tm3assbeh/ m3asbeen? ليع مغَصّب/ مِغَصبي/ مِغَصبين
When are you traveling?	eimtan mseifar/ mseifra/ mseifreen? أمتَن مسافَر/ مسافرَة/ مسافرين
Who is coming to the party?	meen jeyeh 3al sahra? مين جلي على سَهرَة

How are you today?	keefak/ keefik/ keefkoun el yom? كيفَك/ كيفِك/ كيفكُن
How is your father?	keefo bayyak/ bayyik/ baykoun? كيفو بيّك/ بيّك/ بيكُن
How is your mother?	keefa emmak/ emmik/ emkoun? كيفا إمَّك/ إمِك/ إمكُن
How are your children?	keefoun wleidak/ wlei-dik/ wleidkoun? كيفُن ولادَك/ ولادِك/ ولادكُن
What is wrong with you?	shou beik/ bekeh/ bek-oun? شو باك/ بكي/ بكُن
Where are you going?	wein rayiH/ rayHa/ ray-Heen? وَين رايح/ رايحا/ رايحين
What are these mugs for?	la shou hawdeh el kebbei-yeit? أَشو هَودي الكبايات

14

Since when do you wear black?	min emtan btelbous/ btelbseh/btelbso aswad?
	مِن أمتَن بتلبُس/ بتلبسي/ بتلبسوا أسوَد
What else do you suggest?	shou kamein btoktoriH/ btoktorHeh/ btoktorHo?
	شو كَمان بتُقطُرح/ بتُقطُرحي/ بتُقطُرحوا
How come you are here?	keef ta enta/enteh/ento hon?
	كيف تَ إنتَ،/ إنتِ/ إنتو هون
How much does it cost?	addeh Ha'o/ Ha'a/ Ha'oun?
	أدّي حَقّو/ حَقّا/ حَقُّن

15

CHAPTER 2: CONJUGATION

I definitely hated conjugation at school. This is why I only chose to conjugate some pretty awesome verbs: to travel and to love. I believe that if we are constantly in love and visiting new places, then we are pretty close to finding happiness! In summer, Beirut international airport always witnesses high traffic of tourists and expatriates alike. If you haven't visited Lebanon yet, you really should plan a trip soon! Therefore I tell you

Tousal/ tousale bil salemeh (arrive safely!)

Hamdella 3al salemeh (Glad you arrived safely)

Songs: wein msafer, Julia Botros

TO LOVE

ana bHebb

I love

أنا بحبّ

You love	enta betHebb/enteh betHebbeh
	إنتَ بتحبّ/ إنتِ بتحبّي
He loves	howeh biHebb
	هوّ بِحبّ
She loves	hiyyeh betHebb
	هيّ بتحبّ
We love	neHna menHebb
	نِحنا منحبّ
You love	ento betHebbo
	إنتو بتحبّو
They love	henneh biHebbo
	هنّي بحبّو
I loved	ana Habbeit
	أنا حَبيت
You loved	enta Habbeit/enteh Habbayteh
	إنتَ حَبيت/ إنتِ حَبيتي

| He loved | howeh Habb |
| | هوّ حَبّ |

| She loved | hiyeh Habbit |
| | هيّ حَبّت |

| We loved | neHna Habbayna |
| | نحنا حَبينا |

| You loved | ento Habbayto |
| | إنتو حَبيتو |

| They loved | henneh Habbo |
| | هني حَبّو |

| I used to love | ana kenet Hebb |
| | أنا كنت حبّ |

| You used to love | enta kenet tHebb/enteh kenteh tHebbeh |
| | إنتَ كنت تحبّ/ إنتِ كنتِ تحبّي |

| He used to love | howeh kein yHebb |
| | هوّ كان يحبّ |

She used to love	hiyyeh keinit tHebb
	هيّ كانت تحبّ
We used to love	neHna kenna nHebb
	نحنا كنّا نحبّ
You used to love	ento kento tHebbo
	إنتو كنتو تحبّو
They used to love	henneh keino yHebbo
	هنّي كانو يحبّو
I will love	ana raH Hebb
	أنا رَح حبّ
You will love	enta raH tHebb/enteh raH tHebbeh
	إنتَ رَح تحبّ/ إنتي رَح تحبّي
He will love	howeh raH yHebb
	هوّ رَح يحبّ
She will love	hiyeh raH tHebb
	هيّ رَح تحبّ

We will love	neHna raH nHebb
	نحنا رَح نحب
You will love	ento raH tHebbo
	إنتو رَح تحبّو
They will love	henneh raH yHebbo
	هِنّي رَح يحبّوا
I used to love you when we were kids	ana kenet Hebbak lamma kenna wleid
	أنا كنت حبَّك/ حبِّك لَمّا كنا ولاد
He says he loves me like before	howeh bi'oul enno bi-Hebneh metel abel
	هوّ بقول إنّو بحبني متل قَبل
I'm sure you'll love Byblos when you go there	ana akeedeh raH tHebb Jbeil bas trouH/ trouHeh/trouHo
	أنا أكيد/ أكيدة رَح تحبّ جبيل بس تروح/ رح تحبّي جبيل بَس تروحي

TO TRAVEL

I travel	ana bseifir / انا بسافِر
You travel	enta btseifir/ enteh bt-seifreh / إنتَ بتسافِر/ إنتِ بتسافري
He travels	houwweh biseifir / هُوّ بسافِر
She travels	hiyyeh btseifir / هِيّ بتسافِر
We travel	neHna mnseifir / نِحنا منسافِر
You travel	ento btseifro / إنتو بتسافرو
They travel	henneh biseifro / هِنّي بسافرو
I'm traveling	ana mseifar/ mseifra / أنا مسافِر/ مسافرَة

21

| You're traveling | enta mseifar/ enteh mseifra |
| | إنتَ مسافِر/ إنتِ مسافرَة |

| He's traveling | houwweh mseifar |
| | هُوّ مسافَر |

| She's traveling | hiyyeh mseifra |
| | هِيّ مسافرَة |

| We're traveling | neHna mseifreen |
| | نحنا مسافرين |

| You're traveling | ento mseifreen |
| | إنتو مسافرين |

| They're traveling | henneh mseifreen |
| | هِنّي مسافرين |

| I traveled | ana seifaret |
| | أنا سافَرت |

| You traveled | enta seifaret/ enteh seifarteh |
| | إنتَ سافَرت/ إنتِ سافَرتي |

He traveled	houwweh seifar
	هُوّ سافَر
She traveled	hiyyeh seifarit
	هِيّ سافَرت
We traveled	neHna seifarna
	نِحنا سافَرنا
You traveled	ento seifarto
	إنتو سافَرتو
They traveled	henneh seifaro
	هِنّي سافَرو
I used to travel	ana kenet seifir
	أنا كنت سافِر
You used to travel	houwweh kein yseifir/ hiyyeh kenit tseifir
	إنتَ كنت تسافِر/ إنتِ كنتِ تسافري
He used to travel	houwweh kein yseifir
	هُوّ كان يسافِر

She used to travel	hiyyeh keinit tseifir هِيّ كانِت تسافِر
We used to travel	neHna kenna nseifir نِحنا كِنّا نسافِر
You used to travel	ento kento tseifro إنتو كنتو تسافرو
They used to travel	henneh keino yseifro هِنّي كانو يسافرو
I'll travel	ana raH seifir أنا رَح سافِر
You'll travel	enta raH tseifir/ enteh raH tseifreh إنتَ رَح تسافِر/ إنتِ رَح تسافري
He'll travel	houwweh raH yseifir هُوَ رَح يسافِر
She'll travel	hiyyeh raH tseifir هِيّ رَح تسافِر

We'll travel	neHna raH nseifir
	نِحنا رَح نسافِر
You'll travel	ento raH tseifro
	إنتو رَح تسافرو
They'll travel	henneh raH yseifro
	هِنّي رَح يسافرو
I'm traveling to Paris today	ana mseifar/ mseifra 3ala beireez el yom
	أنا مسافَر/ مسافرَة عَلى باريز اليوم
I travel every summer	ana bseifir kel seif/ sayfiyyeh
	أنا بسافِر كِل صَيف/ صَيفيّة
Both my father and my brother, traveled to Brazil last month	khayyeh w bayyeh, seifaro el shaher el madeh 3ala el brazeel
	خَيّ و بَيّ، سافَروا الشَهر الماضي، عَلى البرازيل

25

We used to travel every year	neHna kenna nseifir kel seneh
	نِحنا كِنّا نسافِر كِلّ سنة
When will you travel?	eimtan raH tseifro?
	أمتَن رَح تسافرو؟

CHAPTER 3: AT HOME

Home! So what is it like living in a Lebanese home? No matter the class you come from, your weekly homemade menu would most certainly be made of Mjadra (lentils and cooked rice) and loubiyeh bi zeit (green beans in oil) on weekdays and Macheiweh (barbecue-meat, chicken and the like) on weekends. And yes family does come first. On Sundays, you are bound to invite your teta and jeddo, khalo and 3ammo (grand-parents and uncles) if they haven't sent you the invite first. I for one, usually fast on Saturday night so I can eat all the good stuff on Sunday!

Sahtein (Bon appétit)

Songs: beyti ana baytak, Feyrouz
             beit sghir bi Canada, Feyrouz

INSIDE THE HOUSE

	beit
Home	
	بَيْت

Building	bineyeh
	بناية
Floor	tabe'/ tawabe'
	طَابِق/ طَوابِق
Bedroom	oudit el nom
	قوضِة النَوْم
Living room	oudit el a3deh
	قوضِة القَعْدِة
Kitchen	matbakh
	مَطبَخ
Bathroom	Hemmem
	حَمَام
Bed	takhet
	تَخْت
Closet	khzeineh
	خُزانة
Clothes	tyeib
	تياب

Towel	manshafeh
	مَنْشَفة
Soap	saboun
	صابون
Oven/bakery	foren
	فُرن
Sink	majla
	مَجْلى
Dish	saHen
	صَحْن
Fork	shawkeh
	شَوْكِة
Knife	sekkeen
	سِكّين
Spoon	mal3a'a
	مَلْعقة
Cup	kebbeyeh
	كَبَاية

Couches	kanabeyeh
	كَنَبايِة
Table(s)	tawleh/ tawleit
	طَاوْلِة/ طاولات
Chair(s)	kerseh/ karaseh
	كِرسي/ كَراسِي
On which floor is your apartment?	bi ayya tabe' enta 3ayesh/ enteh 3aysheh?
	بأيِّ طابِق إنتَ عايِش/ إنتِ عايشِي؟
What are you cooking?	shou 3am totbokh/ totbkheh?
	شو عَم تُطبُخ/ تُطبخي؟
I wash my face in the morning	el sobeH bghassil wejjeh
	الصُبُح بغَسِّل وِجَّي
How many times a day do you brush your teeth?	kam marra btfarsheh sneinak/ sneinik/ sneinkoun bil nhar?
	كَم مَرَّة بتفَرشي سنانَك/ سنانِك/ سنانكُن بالنهار؟

In the morning we go to the bakery to buy manakeesh	el sobeH mnrouH 3al foren ta neshtreh mne'eesh الصُبُح مِنروح عَلى قُرن تَنِشتِري مْناقيش
I'm washing the dishes	ana 3am bejleh el sHoun أنا عَم بِجلي الصحون

ORDERING FOOD

| I would like to | badde |
| | بدّي |

| Street | sheri3 |
| | شارع |

| Floor | tabi' |
| | طابِق |

| Facing | bi wejj |
| | بِ وجّ |

| Near | Hadd |
| | حَدّ |

| Ask about | s'al 3ann |
| | سأل عنّ |

| Chicken | djeij |
| | دجاج |

| Garlic | toum |
| | توم |

Pickles	kabees
	كَبيس
With	ma3
	مَع
Without	bala
	بَلا
Extra	zyeideh
	زيادي
Cheese	jebneh
	جِبنة
Vegeterian	nabeiteh
	نَباتي
Ingredients	moukawwineit
	مُكوّنات
Mushrooms	foter
	فُطُر
To add	tzid
	تزيد

To remove	tshil
	تشيل
Mustard	khardal
	خَردَل
Dressing	salsa
	صَلصَة
Light	khafeef
	خَفيف
Cost/ Price	Ha'/ se3er
	حَقّ/ سِعر
I would like to order some food	baddeh otloub akel/tal-abiyyeh
	بَدّي أُطلُب أَكل/ طَلَبيّة
Where should it be delivered to?	la wein mnwassela?
	لَ وَين مِنوصّلا
St Lourdes street, on the fifth floor	ana 3aysheh bi sheri3 st lourde, bil tabi' el khamis
	أنا عايشي بشارع سانت لورد، بالطابِق الخامِس

I want a chicken sandwich without garlic, with pickles, extra hummus	baddeh 3arous djeij, bala toum, ma3 kabees, Hommous extra
	بَدّي عَروس دجاج، بَلا توم، مَع كبيس، أكسترا حُمَص
I want to order three pizza pepperoni, extra cheese	baddeh otloub tleiteh pizza pepperoni, zyedeh jebneh
	بَدّي أُطلُب تلاتي بيتزا بيروني زيادي جِبنة
Do you have vegetarian pizza	3andak/3andik/3andkoun pizza nabetiyeh
	عَندَك/عَنِدِك/عَندكُن بيتزا نباتيّة
What are the toppings of the pizza?	shou btHot/ btHotteh/ btHotto fiya (or bi alba)
	شو بُحُطّ/ بتحُطّي/ بتحُطّوا فيها (بِ قَلبا)
Can you remove the mushrooms	feek tshilleh/ feekeh tshileeleh/ feekoun tshilouleh el foter
	فيك تشلّلي/ فيكي تشيليلي/ فيكُك تشيلولي الفُطُر

Can you add mustard	feek tzeed/ feekeh tzee-deh/ feekoun tzeedo khardal فيك تزيد/ فيكي تزيدي/ فيكُن تزيدو خَردَل
I want to change the dressing	baddeh ghayir el salsa بدّي غَيِّر الصَلصَة
Do you have anything light to order?	shou 3andkoun shi kha-feef (for a group of peo-ple) شو عَندكُن شي خَفيف
Today's special	taba' el yom طَبَق اليوم
What is today's special?	shou taba' el yom شو طَبَق اليوم
When will the food be ready?	ade bado wa'et el akel ta yousal أَدَي بَدَو وَقت الأكل تَ يوصَل
How much will the food cost	addeh byotla3 Ha' el akel? أَدَي بِيطلَع حَقّ الأكل

WINTER

Winter	shiteh
	شِتي
Cold	sa'3a
	سَقعَة
Storm	3asfeh
	عَاصِفة
Snow	talej
	تَلج
Road	taree'
	طَريق
Electric heater	deffeiyeh
	دِفاية
Chimney	maw'adeh/ shemineh
	شوميني
Coal	Hatab
	حَطَب

Winter food	akel el shiteh
	أكل الشِتِي

Chestnut	kastana
	كَستنا

Grilled potatoes	batata meshwiyeh
	بطاطا مِشويّة

Soup	shawraba
	شَوَرَبَة

Scarf	sheil
	شال

Gloves	kfouf
	كفوف

Hat	bornayta
	بُرنَيطَة

Coat	kabbout
	كَبّوت

It's really cold today	el yom, kteer sa'3a
	اليوم، كنير سَقعَة
There is a storm coming soon	fi 3asfeh jeiyeh areeban
	في عاصِفِة جايي قَريبًا
It snowed yesterday	talajit mbeiriH
	تَلَجِت مبارِح
The road was blocked	el taree' kein ma'tou3/ msakkar
	الطَريق كان مَقطوع/ مسَكَّر
It's too cold, i can't go out, I don't want to catch a cold	kteer sa'3a, ma feeneh odhar, ta ma omrad
	كتير سَقعَة، ما فِيني أُضهَّر، تَ ما أمرَض
Heaters	wasei'il tadfi'a
	وَسائِل تَدفِءة
I am going to the mountains to see the snow	ana rayHa/ rayiH 3al talej
	انا رايحل على تَلج

I am going skiing	ana rayHa/ rayiH a3moul ski
	أنا رايحا أعمُل سكي
Keep warm	tddaffeh/ tdaffa/ tdaffo mniH
	تدَفَّى/ تدفّي/ تدفّوا منيح

CHAPTER 4: WORK AND STUDYING

For me, unlike school, university has been a really fun time. After all, I studied drama! In Lebanon, children go to school for 15 years starting at age 3. Lebanon once again offers various top-notch schools and universities that provide high quality education.

As for work, it is certainly not very easy to find a job here! Demands obviously exceed offers leading thus to increasing immigration.

Ya3tik/ ya3tikeh el 3afyeh (after someone finishes any kind of physical or intellectual task).

Songs: chtegil w ma to'bad ya Habboub, Ghassan el Rahbani

STUDYING

Pencil	alam rsas
	قَلَم رصاص

Pen	alam
	قَلَم
Paper	war'a
	وَرقة
I write	bektoub
	بِكتُب
Book	kteib
	كتاب
Notebook	daftar
	دَفتَر
Ruler	mastara
	مَسطَرَة
Board	lawH
	لَوح
Teacher (man)	esteiz
	إستاذ
Teacher (woman)	m3almeh
	معَلمة

I am a student	ana tilmeez/ tilmeezeh أنا تلميذ/ تلميذة
I study Arabic	ana bedrous 3arabeh أنا بدرُس عَرَبي
I study at the Lebanese university	ana bedrous bil jeim3a el lebneiniyeh أنا بدرُس بالجامعة اللّبنانيّة
I am a student of Arabic at the Lebanese university	ana telmeez/telmeezeh, w bedrous 3arabeh bil jeim3a el lebneiniyeh أنا تلميذ/تلميذة، وبدرُس عَرَبي بالجامعة اللّبنانيّة
I write on a paper using a pen	ana bektoub bil alam 3ala el war'a أنا بِكتُب بالقَلَم عَلى الوَرقَة
May I go to the bathroom	fineh rouH 3al Hemmeim فيني روح عَلى حَمّام
Can you lend me your pen?	feek t3eerneh/ feekeh t3ireeneh/ feekoun t3irouneh alam? فيك تعيرني قَلَم/ فيكي تعيريني قَلَم/ فيكُن تعيروني قلَم

43

JOBS

	sheghel
Job	شغل
	ashghal
Jobs	اشغال
	kindarjeh
Cobbler	كِندَرجي
	Heddeid
Blacksmith	حِدّاد
	najjar
Carpenter	نَجّار
	mecanisiein
Mechanic	ميكانيسيان
	dikkein
Grocery store	دِكّان
	dikkanjeh
Grocery-man	دِكّنجي

Vegetables	khodra خُضرَة
Greengrocer	khadarjeh خَضَرجي
Garden	jnayneh جنَينة
Gardener	jnayneiteh جنيناتي
Bread	khebez خِبز
Bread maker/ baker	khebbeiz / forran خِبّاز/ فُرّان
Hairdresser	Hellei'/ coiffeur جلّاق/ جلّاقَة
Fortune teller	bossar/ bossara بصّار/ بَصّارَة
House painter	torrash طُرّاش

Tiles	**blat**
	بلاط

Tiler	bollat
	بُلاّط

Electrician	**kahrabjeh**
	كَهرَبجي

Doorman	natour
	ناطور

Tailor	**khiyyat/ khiyyata**
	خِيّاط/ خِياطَة

CHAPTER 5: BODY AND DOCTORS

Not a happy chapter hein? But hey, think about the cure not the illness. There is at least one doctor in every family. Not only is it a source of pride for every extended family member, but also a national glorification. Lebanese doctors have indeed excelled in various domains. Plastic surgery makes no exception, it actually gave birth to medical tourism whereas many arrive to our capital in the hope of leaving it looking even prettier!

3a salemeh then (may you have a fast and easy recovery)

Songs:

Saydali ya saydali , Azar Habib (saydali means pharmacist)

Tabib garraH, Georges Wassouf (tabib is another word for doctor)

BODY

Body	jesem
Body	جِسم

47

Face	**wejj**
	وِجّ
Eyebrows	**Hweijib**
	حواجِب
Nose	**menkhar/mankhour**
	مِنخار/مَنخور
Eye	**3ayn**
	عَين
Eyes	**3youn**
	عيون
Eyelashes	**rmoush**
	رموش
Mouth	**temm**
	تِمّ
Cheek	**khadd**
	خَدّ
Cheeks	**khdoud**
	خدود

Hair	sha3er
	شَعر
Neck	ra'beh
	رَقبة
Chest/breast	soder
	صُدر
Shoulders	kteif
	كتاف
Arm	eed
	إيد
Stomach	me3deh
	مِعدة
Belly	baten
	بَطن
Hips	wrak
	وراك
Waist	khaser
	خَصر

Leg	ejer
	إجر
Legs	ejrein
	إجرين
Knee	rekbeh
	ركبة
Fingers	asabe3
	أصابع
Toes	asabe3 el ejrein
	أصابع الإجرين
Head	ras
	راس
Ear	dayneh
	دَينه
Ears	dinein
	دينَين
Mole	shemiyeh
	شاميّة

Tooth	sinn سِنّ
Teeth	snein سنان
Tongue	lsein لسان
Lip	shiffeh شِفّه
Lips	shfeif شفاف
My body hurts	jesmeh 3am youja3neh جسمي عَم يوجَعني
This girl has long hair	heydeh el benet sha3ra taweel هيدي البنت شعرا طويل
This boy has long hair	heyda el sabeh sha3ro aseer هيدا الصبي شعرو طويل

I have a headache	raseh 3am youja3neh
	راسي عم يوجعني
This girl is so skinny	heydeh el benet kteer d3ifeh
	هيدي البنت كتير ضعيفه
This boy is overweight	heyda el sabeh naseH
	هيدا الصَبي ناصِح

DOCTOR

Advice	nasiHa
	نَصيحَة
Cause	sabab?
	سَبَب
Hereditary	wirateh
	وراتي
Medicine	dawa
	ذَوا
Medicines	edewyeh
	إدوية
I'm sick	ana mareed/ mareeda sakhin/ sakhneh
	أنا مَريض/ مَريضَة صاخِن/ صاخنة
I'm feeling tired	ana te3bein/ te3beineh
	أنا تعبان/ تعبانة
I want to see a doctor	baddeh shouf Hakeem/ Hakeemeh
	بَدّي شوف حَكيم/ حَكيمة

Can you recommend a good doctor	feek tonsaHneh/ feekeh tonsaHeeneh bi Hakeem/ Hakeemeh shatir/ shatra
	فيك تُنصَحني بحكيم شاطِر/ فيكي تُنصَحيني بحَكيمي شاطرَة
I feel pain in my stomach	Hasis/ Hasseh bi waja3 bi me3dteh
	حاسِس/ حاسّي بِوَجَع بمعدتي
I have a headache	raseh 3am youja3neh
	راسي عَ يوجَعني
My arm hurts	eedeh 3am touja3neh
	إدي عَم توجَعني
Doctor, is it something serious (dangerous)?	Hakeem, fi shi khotir?
	حَكيم، في شي خُطِر؟
What's causing me this pain?	shou yalleh 3am bisabbebleh hal waja3?
	شو يَلّي عَم بِسبّبلي هَل وَجَع
Is there a solution/ treatment?	fi Hall/ 3ileij?
	في حَلّ/ عِلاج

Are there more tests to be done?	leizim a3moul ba3ed fHousat?
	لازِم أعمُل بَعد فحوصات؟
Is surgery necessary?	bte3te'id/ bte3te'deh lezim a3moul 3amaliyeh?
	بتعتقّد/ بتعتقدي لازِم أعمُل عَمَليّة؟
Tell me what you are feeling	khabberneh shou Hassis/ khabreeneh shou Hasseh
	خَبّرني شو حاسِس/ خَبريني شو حاسّي
Where does it hurt?	wein 3am youja3ak/ you-ja3ik?
	وَين عَم يوجَعَك/ يوجَعِك؟
How long have you been feeling this pain?	addeh sarlo el waja3 (addeh sarlak mawjou3/ mawjou3a)?
	أدّي صَرلو الوَجَع (أدّي صَرلَك (موجوع/ موجوعَة
Is it something common in your family	hal hayda shi wirateh bi 3ayltak/ 3ayltik?
	هَل هَيدا شي وِراتي بعَيلتَك/ عيلتِك؟

55

Do you have any chronic disease?	3andak/ 3andik amrad mouzmineh?
	عَندَك/ عندِك أمراض مُزمِنة؟
Do you have any kind of allergies?	3andak/ 3andik Haseisiyeh 3a shi?
	عَندَك/ عَندِك حَساسِيّة عَشي؟
Take this medicine three times per day	khod/ khedeh el dawa tleit marrat bil nhar
	خود/ خِدي الدَوا تلات مَرّات بالنهار

CHAPTER 6: POLITICS

I definitely dislike this chapter. Nowadays Politics mean war, agonizing kids, terrorism, world hunger and every other atrocity one can think of...It goes without saying that Lebanese politics leave much to envy as means of conducting a country!

Wishing for peace and peace only.

PART 1

Politics	**siyeiseh**
	سياسِة
Country	**balad**
	بَلَد
Capital	**3aasmeh**
	عاصمة

State	dawleh/wileiyeh
	دَولة/ وِلاية

President	ra'ees/ra'eeseh
	رَئيس/ة

King	malik
	مَلِك

Queen	malikeh
	مَلِكة

Republic	joumhouriyeh
	جُمهورِيَة

Kingdom	mamlakeh
	مَملَكِة

Parliament	barlamein
	بَرلَمان

Ministry	wizara
	وزارَة

Minister	wazeer
	وَزير

Ministers	wouzara / وُزَرا
Representative	neiyib / نايِب
Representatives	nouwweib / نُوّاب
Nation	oummeh / أُمّة
Party	Hezeb / حِزب
Parties	aHzeib / أحزاب
Elections	intikhabeit / إنتِخابات
Revolution	sawra / ثَورَة
The capital of Lebanon is Beirut	3aasmit lebnein, beirut / عاصِمِة لبنان, بَيروت

Republic of Lebanon	joumhouriyet lebnein/ el joumhouriyeh el lebneiniyeh جُمهوريّة لبنان/ الجُمهوريّة اللّبنانيّة
United nations	el oumam el meteHdeh الأُمَم المِتّحْدة
Today, the representatives met at the parliament to elect a president	el yom, el nouwweib jtama3o bil barlamein ta yentekhbo ra'ees اليوم, النوّاب جتمعوا تينتخبوا رئيس
There are two main political parties in the United States	fi Hezbein aseisiyyeh bil wileiyeit el metteHdeh في حِزبين أساسيّة بالولايات المِتّحْدة

PART 2

Municipality/ies	baladiyyeh/ baladiyyeit
	بَلَدِيّة/ بَلَدِيّات
Peace	saleim
	سَلام
Peaceful	selmiyyeh
	سِلميّة
Protest	mouzahara
	مُظاهَرَة
Protests	mouzaharat
	مُظاهَرات
Martyr	shaheed
	شهيد
There is a garbage crisis in Lebanon, and the government did not find a solution yet.	fi azmit nifeiyeit bi lebnen, wl Hkoumeh ba3ed ma le'yit Hall
	في أزمِة نِفايات بِلبنان، والحكومِة بَعد ما لقيت حَلّ

61

| Every municipality is responsible for sorting and recycling waste | kel baladiyyeh, mas'ouleh 3an farez el nifeiyeit |
| | كِلّ بَلَدِيّة، مَسؤولِة عَن فرز النِفايات |

| There are ongoing peaceful protests in the Lebanese capital demanding the resignation of the minister of the environment | fi mouzaharat selmiyyeh moustamerra bil 3asmeh el lebneniyeh, 3am bettalib bi esti'alit wazeer el bee'a |
| | في مُظاهرات سِلميّة مُستمرّة بالعاصمة اللبنانية، عَم بطالِب بإستقالة وَزير البيئة |

| Today, fifty people were killed after an explosion | el yom, khamseen shakhes meito nateejit enfijar |
| | اليَوم، خَمسين شَخص ماتوا نَتيجة إنفجار |

| In 2013, the parliament amended the constitution extending thus their term | bil alfein w tleta3sh, majlis el nouwweib 3addalo el doustour, ta ye'daro ymaddido la nafsoun |
| | بِل ألفين وتلاتعش مَجلِس النّواب عَدَّلوا الدُستور، تَ يقدَروا يمَدّدوا لَ نَفسُن |

CHAPTER 7: FORMALITIES

Ah formalities... This is definitely a chapter that all Lebanese are very familiar with. We've been raised hearing a lot of "3ayb" (fault/disgrace), of kellak zo2 (you're full of good manners), of iza ma fi te2leh (if it's not too much to ask)...

Lebanese are attached to traditions. Some are still very pleasant to see: standing up when someone walks in or out of a room, visiting your grandparents every week, walking with your guest to the door and staying a few or long moments saying goodbye and 're'-catching up... I still remember as a kid, searching for my mother only to find her 30 minutes later at the door still conversing with her favorite neighbor Tante Rita!

Nowadays, a lot of this happens through social media, including a visit to your grandparents...

AT THE DOOR

Good luck	mwaffa'/ mwaffa'a/ mwaffa'een موَفَق/ موَفَقَة/ موَفَقين
Godspeed	ma3 el saleimeh مَع السّلامة
Why don't you stay?	khalleek/ khalleekeh/ khalleekoun خَلّيك/ خَلّيكي/ خَلّيكُن
Stay a little longer	khalleek (b'a) ba3d shwey خَلّيك (بقا) بَعد شوي
God be with you	allah ma3ak/ ma3ik/ ma3koun الله مَعَك/ مَعِك/ مَعكُن
Pass by soon	teb'a toll/ teb'eh tolleh/ teb'o tollo تبقَ طُلّ/ تبقي طُلّي/ تبقو طُلّو
Why don't you pass by?	mayyil/ mayleh/ maylo مَيِّل/ مَيلي/ مَيلو

Do come again	3eeda/ 3idiya/ 3idouwa
	عيدا/ عيديا/ عيدووا
Where are you going?	la wein?
	لوين؟
Do come again: (for individuals and groups alike)	min3adeh
	مِنعادة
Goodnight	sa3eedeh/ tosbaH 3a kheir
	سَعيدة/ تُصبَح ع خَير
Goodnight (as a reply to the above)	w enta/enteh/ ento min ahlo
	و إنتَ/ إنتِ/ إنتو من أهلو
Say hi to...	sallim/ salmeh/ salmo
	سَّلِّم/ سَلمي/ سَلمو
Will do	wosil
	وُصِل
OK, i have to go	yalla, sar lezim emsheh
	يَلا صار لازم إمشي

65

We have to leave (Literal Translation: "OK, we saw you")	yalla shefneikoun
	يلّا شفناكُن
Is there anything I can do before I leave?	baddak, baddik, badkoun shi?
	بَدَّك/ بَدِّك/ بَدكُن شي؟
We're happy to have seen you	mbasatna shefneikoun
	مبسَطنا شفناكُن
We will come again	min3eeda gheir marra
	منعيدا غَير مَرّا

MANNERS

3mol/3meleh ma3rouf

عمول/ عميلي مَعروف

min fadlak/ min fadlik

مِن فَضلَك/ فَضلِك

Bi sharafak/bi sharafik

بِشَرَفَك/ بِشَرَفِك

Please

ma tosghar

ما تُصغَر

iza btreed/ btreedeh

إذا بتريد/ بتريدي

	3afwan
	عَفْوًا
	b3azbak/b3azbik
	بعَزبَك/ بعَزبِك
	law samaHet/ law samaHteh
Excuse me	لَو سَمَحت/ لَو سَمَحتي
	ma twekhezneh/ ma twekhzeeneh
	ما تواخزني/ تواخزيني
	min ba3ed eznak/ eznik
	مِن بَعد إذنَك/ إذنِك

tekram 3aynak/3aynik

تكرَم عَينَك/ عَينِك

tekram / tekrameh
تِكرَم/ تِكرَمي

ahla

أهلا

ya 3eib el shoum
يا عَيب الشوم

la 3younak/ 3younik

لَعيونَك/ لَعيونِك

You're welcome

mish bayneitna
مِش بيناتنا

walaw

وَلَو

Don't mention it

	yeslamo
	يِسلَمو
	ysallemoun
	يسلّمُن
	teslam
	تِسلَم
	yeslamo hal idein
	يسلَمو هَل إدين
Thank you	**shoukran**
	شُكرًا
	mashkour / mashkoura
	مَشكور/ مَشكورَة
	kellak/ kellik zo'
	كِلَك/ كِلِك زوق
	khajjaltna/ khajjalteena
	خَجَلتِنا/ خَجَلتينا

Salutation/ hope to find you well	**ykhaleelna yeik/ yeikeh**
	يخَليلنا ياك
	ykhaleek/ ykhaleekeh fo' rasna
	يخلَيك/ يخَلَيكي فوق راسنا
	allah yoHfazak
	الله يُحفظَك/ يُحفظك
	allah ykhalleek
	الله يخَلَيك/ يخَلَيكي
	ya3teek/ ya3teekeh el 3afyeh
	يَعطيك/ يَعطيكي العافية
	allah y3afeek/ y3afeekeh
	الله يعافيك/ يعافيكي

Your wish is my command	**b amrak/ b amrik** بِأَمرَك
Is it ok?	**ma3leh iza?** مَعلي إذا؟
Do you have any problem with that?	**3andak/3andik meshkleh?** عَندَك/ عَندِك مشكلة؟
No problem	**mish meshkleh** مِش مشكلة
It doesn't matter	**ma bi'assir** ما بأَثَر

CHAPTER 8: MISCELLANEOUS

The word extra is used a lot in daily situations. Especially when ordering street food you would say: I want one faleifil, with extra tarator (taHini dressing)

Baddeh waHad faleifil, tarator extra.

Now this chapter sheds light on "soccer". And when it comes to soccer, Lebanese take it pretty seriously. Our two most popular football teams are el nejmeh (the star) and el ansar (the fans) both based in Beirut. International championships barely leave any Lebanese neutral. Fans are highly supportive of either the Brazilian or the German team... Restaurants, Cafés and every single balcony would be stacked with people watching the game and cheering their favorite players while wearing the full (authentic or not) team's uniform of course. Celebrations will then follow throughout the night with fans honking cars making as much noise as possible so that no adversary shall ever find sleep again!

Wazzeklo (when you make fun of the other team's fans because they lost)

Mabrouk: to congratulate the fans of the team that won.

Songs: mabrouk mabrouk, Rami Ayyach

WORLD CUP

Team	faree'	
	فَريق	
Player/s	lei3ib/lei3beh/la3eebeh	
	لاعِب/الاعبي/ لَعيبي	
I'm with	ana ma3	
	أنا مَع	
I'm against	ana dodd	
	أنا ضُد	
Gain	rebeH	
	ربح	
Loss	khsara	
	خسارَة	
Spanish team	faree' espaneh	
	فَريق إسباني	
Brazilian team	faree' brazeeleh	
	فَريق برازيلي	

Italian team	faree' telyeineh (or italeh)
	فَريق طلياني/ إطالي
German team	faree' almaneh
	فَريق ألماني
French team	faree' faranseh (or frenseiweh)
	فَريق فَرَنسي/ فرنساوي
World cup	ka'es el 3alam/ mondial
	كأس العالَم
What's your favorite team?	enta/enteh ma3 ayya faree'/ aya faree' btshaji3/btshaj3eh
	إنتَ/إنتِ أيّا فريق بتشَجِّع/ بتشَجِّعي
This year, the world cup is in Brazil	heydeh el seneh, ka'es el 3alam bil brazeel
	هَيدي السنة، كأس العالم بالبرازيل
Four years ago, it was in South Africa	min arba3 sneen, kein bi afree'ya el jnoubiyeh
	مِن أربَع سنين، كان بأفريقيا الجنوبيّة

She supports the Spanish team	hiyeh ma3 el faree' el espaneh هيّ مَع الفَريق الأسباني
This year I won't cheer for any team	heydeh el seneh, ana manneh ma3 wala faree' هَيدي السنة، أنا مَنّي مَع ولا فَريق
My team will win	faree'eh raH yerbaH فَريقي رَح يربَح
I hope your team loses	betmanna faree'ak/ faree'ik yekhsar بتمنّى فريقَك/ فَريقِك يخسَر

CHAPTER 9: TEXTS

PRESENT TENSE

First visit to Lebanon

I now arrive to Rafi' el Hariri Airport in Beirut. It's the first time I visit Lebanon. My name is Nora and my father is Lebanese, my mother is English.

Each day my father tells me about Lebanon and about Khyeim, his village in southern Lebanon. I'm so excited to go to the south, but before, I want to explore Beirut.

My friend Maher is waiting for me outside the airport he wants to invite me to lunch at a restaurant in Hamra.

(Nora and Maher in front of the airport)

Nora: Maher! I'm here, I miss you a lot!

Maher: Nora ya Nora, missing you a lot, you finally come to Lebanon! I hope you are hungry because I'm inviting you to the best restaurant in town.

Nora: I'm starving, looking forward!

(In the car)

Nora: Ohhhh, too much traffic! It's been 1 hour on the road!

Maher: yeah it's normal, this is Beirut! It takes you 10 minutes to reach Hamra from the airport at night, but a whole hour during the day!

Nora: and ohhh it's so hot, I'm suffocating!

Maher: if you keep on nagging, I'll throw you outside the car hahaha

(At the restaurant)

Nora: We finally arrive to the restaurant, and my mood drastically changes here! After the hot weather and the traffic I'm going to order Tabbouleh.

Maher: heh, are we just going to eat Tabbouleh? You will see, I'm going to ask for a special meza. Excuse me, we want to order.

Waiter: Go ahead.

Maher: Ok so, we want 1 dish of tabbouleh, 1 dish of spiced potatoes, 1 Hummus, 1 plate of raw sheep's liver, 1 plate of fried kebbeh and of course 2 glasses of 3ara'.

(Nora on the phone)

Hello, good evening dad. I can't tell you how happy I am! I wish you are with me. I'm exercising in Rawche now and partying in Mar Mkhayel later. How's the weather like? Well, too hot but a bit smoother in the evening.

I'm going to Khyeim on Sunday, ok I kiss you and big hello to mom. Love you!

———————————

awwal zyara 3ala lebnein

ana halla' wsolet 3a matar rafee' el Hariri Beirut. heydeh awwal marra bzour lebnein. esmeh nora w bayyeh lebneineh, emmeh engliziyeh.

bayyeh kel yom bikhaberneh 3an lebnein w 3an day3to bil khyeim bi jnoub lebnein. ana kteer mHammasseh rouH 3al jnoub, bas abel baddeh ekteshif beirut.

rfee'eh maher naterneh barrat el matar, baddo ye3zemneh 3al

ghada bi mat3am bil Hamra.

(nora w maher eddeim el matar)

nora: maher! ana hon, shta'tellak kteer!

maher: nora ya nora! meshta'lik kteer, akheeran jeeteh 3ala lebnein! yalla nshala tkouneh je3aneh l'en 3eizmik 3a atyab mat3am bil
balad

nora: mkhawra! badeh el sarfeh ousal!

(bil siyara)

nora: ufffff, shou fi 3aj'a! sarlna sei3a 3al taree' !

maher : eh shi tabee3eh, heydeh beirut ! min el matar lal Hamra
baddik 3asher d'ayi' bil leil, bas bil nhar sei3a !

nora : w ufff shou fi shob, ftoset !

maher : iza raH tdalleh tne'eh, bkebbik min el siyara hahahaha

(bil mat3am)

nora: akheeran wsolna 3al mat3am, tghayarit nafseeteh. min ba3ed
el shob wl 3aj'a, raH otloub tabbouleh.

maher: heh, bas raH neikoul tabbouleh? halla' btshoufeh, raH
otloub mezza gheir shikel. 3afwan, badna notloub.

waiter: yalla tfaddal

maher: tayyib, badna saHen tabbouleh, saHen batata Harra, wa-
Had Hommous, saHen asbeh nayyeh, w sahen kebbeh me'liyeh w
akeed keisein 3ara' 3ala zaw'ak

(nora 3al telephone)

- allo masa el kheir baba. ma bkhabrak addeh mabsouta ana!
ya reit enta ma3eh! ana hala' 3al rawsheh 3am ba3moul riyada w
ba3dein rayHa osshar bi mar mkhayel. keef el ta'es? shob kteer
kteer bas bil leil fi shwey broud aHsan min el nhar.

ana el aHad rayHa 3al khyeim, yalla bbousak w sallim 3ala mama
kteer. bHebbak.

PAST TENSE

Today I woke up at 6.30 in the morning, I drank my coffee, took a shower, got dressed and left home. Since I was going to Achrafieh, I waited for a taxi on the street. When the first one arrived, I told the driver: to Achrafieh, but he answered that he was not going there. I kept waiting till another one came by and I said again: Achrafieh? He replied: servicein (double the charge) Achrafieh is far. I agreed. As I sat down, I paid 4000ll and finally reached my destination. There, I sat at a café that served delicious coffee. I ordered a latte with no sugar and waited for the meeting I had. When the guy arrived, I said: Hello, I am Hiba and he replied: I'm Mohammad. Mohammad and I talked, discussed some issues and agreed to start up our charity organization as of next week. I'll tell you all the details in an up-coming video. We finished the meeting and I felt very hungry. I called my friend and said: Allo, hi Christelle, do you have time for lunch? She said yes, and so we met at an Italian restaurant that serves excellent pizza. I ordered a Margherita and Christelle had a vegetarian. We ate, had a glass of wine, paid the bill then I went home by service while she headed back to work. I reached home, made coffee and sat on the balcony, then felt that the weather is really nice and that spring has started. I drank my coffee and that's how I spent my day. See you soon.

---

el yom w3eet 3al sei3a setteh w noss el sobeH, shrebet ahweh, tHammamet, akalet, lbeset tyeibeh w daharet min el beit. kenet rayHa 3al Ashrafiyeh. w'efet 3al taree' nataret "service". Wosil aw-wal waHad, eltello: "3al Ashrafiyeh?", alleh: "mish wasil". nataret siyyara teinyeh, eltello: "marHaba, 3al Ashrafiyeh?", alleh: "service-in (2 services), el Ashrafiyeh b3eedeh". eltello ok! tlo3et bil siyyara, dafa3tello arba3-t-aleif, w wsolet 3al Ashrafiyeh. honik a3adet bi ahweh, 3anda ahweh taybeh kteer. talabet ahweh bi Haleeb bala sekkar, w nataret el ejtimei3 yalleh kein 3andeh yeh. nataret el zala-meh w wosil eltello: "marHaba ana hiba", alleh: " ahla, ana mHam-mad". Hkeena ana w mHammad w ttafa'na nballich sheghel jdeed el osbou3 li jeiyeh.

ana w mHammad raH neftaH jam3iyyeh khayriyeh, bkhaberkoun 3an el tafaseel bi video teineh. khalasna el ejtimei3 w Hasseit enneh je3aneh kteer. Da'eit la rfee'teh eltella: " allo hi christelle, ma3keh wa'et netghadda ? » aletleh eh !

lta'ayna ana w christelle, bi mat3am telyeineh 3ando pizza taybeh kteer. ana talabet pizza Margherita, w christelle talabit pizza nabe-itiyeh. akalna w shrebna keis nbeed abyad. dafa3na el Hseib, w ana rje3et 3ala beyteh service, w hiyyeh rej3it 3ala sheghla.

wsolet 3al beit, 3melet ahweh, a3adet 3al balcon, w Hasseit eno el ta'es Helo kteer w ballash el rabee3. shrebet ahweh w heik bikoun kholis el nhar lal yom. bshoufkoun areeban!

FUTURE TENSE

Beach tomorrow?
(a dialogue between Yasmine and Salwa)

-Yasmine: How do you think the weather will be tomorrow?

- Salwa: Tomorrow, it may rain. But the day after tomorrow the weather will surely be beautiful and sunny.

- Yasmine: So we'll go to the beach after tomorrow.

- Salwa: Rabih and I can't, we have work. But tomorrow we're taking the day off.

- Yasmine: OK, so we'll go to the beach tomorrow for sure. Do not forget to call Yasmine and ask her if she feels like coming with us.

- Salwa: I will call her later. Who else do you want to invite? Maybe Talal and his family?

- Yasmine: Yes his wife is nice, and that way, his children will play with ours. We will have fun. Who will take us?

- Salwa: We'll take two cars. One group will go with me and another with Talal, if he comes.

- Yasmine: If we tell him that lunch will be fish and Arak, he will come for sure.

- Salwa: So the plan is fixed. It's as if we're traveling! We've been talking about it for a whole week!

- Yasmine: True! OK so I will get moving. What will you do?

- Salwa: I will finish some work before the kids arrive. I want to send an email to a client to show him how work is progressing. Then I will shower and wear my clothes to bring the kids from school. How about you, what are you up to?

- Yasmine: I have work too. And in the afternoon we're going to the mountain, the weather is wonderful now. We will run and maybe we sleep over.

- Salwa: The important thing is that you don't get late for the beach tomorrow.

- Yasmine: Don't worry! Do you need anything?

- Salwa: Thank you!

---

baHer boukra?
(Hiwar bein Yasmine w Salwa)

Yasmine: kif awlik raH ykoun el taeis boukra?

Salwa: boukra ma32oul tchatteh. Bas ba3ed boukra akid el taeis Helo w saHo

Yasmine: laken mnrouH ba3ed boukra 3al baHer

Salwa : Ana w rabi3 ma fina, 3anna chegeil. Bas boukra ekhdin (3anna) forsa

Yasmine : Tayyib kalas, 3al akid boukra mnrouH 3al baHer. Ma tense tde22e la Yasmine tes2aliya iza 3abela teje ma3na.

Salwa : hala2 ba3ed chway btalfenla (bottosil fiya/ behkiya/ bde22ela) ok. Min baddik ne3zoum kamen? barke Talal w 3aylto?

Yasmine: Eh marto lazizeh ktir w heik wledo byel3abo ma3 wled-na (el wleid byel3abo ma3 ba3ed). raH netsalla. Ma3 min mnrouH (raH nrouH)

Salwa : MnrouH siyartein. 2osem ma3e w 2osem ma3 Talal iza eja.

Yasmine: Iza mn2ello el ghada samak w 3ara2 3al akid byeje

Salwa: Laken tamem rekib el machrou3. Uf kaenno msefrin. sarl-na jem3a bi hal sireh (mne7ke 3an el mawdou3)

Yasmine: 3angad! Tayyib (tab) ana raH emche. Chou 3amleh?

Salwa: RaH khalis kam chagleh abeil ma yousalo el wled. bade eb3at emails lal zboun farji wein wsoleit bil chegeil. Ba3dein raH etHammam w elbous ta rouH jiboun (jib el wled) mn el madrase. Ente chou 3amleh?

Yasmine: Ana kamen 3ande chegeil. w ba3ed el doher tal3in 3al jabal, bi3a2id el taeis hala2. RaH nrouH nerkoud w barke mnnem fo2.

Salwa: Mouhem ma tet2akharo 3al baHer boukra. Yalla bchoufik!

Yasmine : Ma te3tale hamm. Baddik chi?

Salwa: Salemtik, bchoufik boukra!

بَحر بُكرا؟
(جوار بَين يَسمين و سَلوَة)

يَسمين: كيف قَولِك رَح يكون الطَقس بُكرا؟

سَلوَة: بُكرا مَعقول تشَتِّي، بَس بَعد بُكرا أكيد الطَقس حِلو و صَحو

يَسمين: لَكان مِنروح بَعد بُكرا على بَحر

سلوة: أنا و رَبيع ما فينا، عَنّا شِغل، بَس بُكرا آخدين فُرصَة

يسمين: طَيِّب خَلَص، على أكيد بُكرا مِنروح على بَحر. ما تِنسي تدقِّي لَيَسمين، تِسأليا إذا عَبالا تجي مَعنا

سلوة: هَلَّء بَعد شوَيِّ بتَلفِنلا أوكي. مين بَدِّك نعزم كَمان؟ بَركي طَلال و عَيلتو؟

يسمين: إي مَرتو لَذيذِة كتير، و هيك ولادو بيلعَبوا مَع ولادنا . رَح نِتسَلّاً. مَع مين مِنروح؟

سلوة: منروح سيّارتين. قُسم مَعي و قُسم مَع طلال إذا إجا

يسمين: إذا منقلُو الغَدا سَمَك و عَرَق، على أكيد بيجي

سلوة: لَكان تَمام، رِكِب المَشروع! أوف كَإنّو مسافرين. صَرلنا جمعَة بِهَل

سيرة

يسمين: عَنجَدًا طَيِّب أنا رَح إمشي، شو عامِلِة؟

سلوة: رَح خَلِّص كَم شَغلِة قَبِل ما يوصَلو الولاد. بَدِّي إبعَت "إميلز" للزبون، فرجي وين وصُلْت بالشِغِل. بَعدين رَح إتحَمَّم و إلبُس تَروح جيبُن من المَدرَسِة. إنتِ شو عامِلِة؟

يسمين: أنا كَمان عَندي شُغِل، و بَعد الضُهُر طالعين على جَبَل. بِعَقِّد الطَقَس هَلَّء. رَح نروح نِركُض و بَركي مِنّام فوق

سلوة: مُهِمّ ما تِتأُخَّروا على بَحر بُكرا

يسمين: ما تِعتِّلي هَمّ. بَدِّك شي؟

سلوة: سلامتِك، بشوفِك بُكرا

84

CHAPTER 10: EXERCISES

EXERCISE NUMBER 1
Fill in the blank:

1.   Where do you live?

       Weyn _____?

2.   When do you want to eat?

       _____ badak _____?

3.   Who are you?

       _____ inta?

4.   Why are you sad?

       _____?

5.   What do you think about these curtains?

       _____ ra'yak bi hal _____?

Answers:

1)	Sekin/ 3ayich	ساكن/ عايش
2)	Emtan badkoun teklo	أمتَن بَدكُن تاكلوا؟
3)	Min	مين
4)	Leh ze3len/ ze3leneh	ليه زعلان/ زعلانة
5)	Chou ra'yak bi hal baradeh	شو رَأيَك بِهَل بَرادي ؟

EXERCISE NUMBER 2

Find the questions to these answers:

1)	Ana men lebnen.	أنا مِن لِبنان
2)	Ana asleh frenseweh / faranseh	أنا أصلي فرنساوي /فرنسي
3)	Ana nejjar.	أنا نِجّار
4)	Ana marid.	أنا مَريض
5)	La2 yeslamo bekhod taxi.	لاء يِسلَمو باخُد تاكسي
6)	Sekin bi Jbeil.	ساكِن بِجبَيل

Answers:

1)	Men weyn inte?	شو جِنسيتَك/ مِن وَين إنت؟
2)	Men weyn inte?	مِن وَين الأصل/أصلك؟
3)	Chou btechteghil?	شو بتشتِغِل؟
4)	Kifak/ beik chi?	كيفَك/باك شي؟
5)	Baddak waslak?	بَدَّك وَصلَك؟
6)	Weyn sekin?	وَين ساكِن

EXERCISE NUMBER 3

Translate:

1. I want to see you tonight

2. I wanted to eat

3. I saw a brown dog yesterday

4. They saw a doctor in the house

5.   You wanted to see the lawyer

_____

Answers:

1)	badeh choufak el layleh	بَدّي شوفَك اللّيلة
2)	ken badeh ekol	أنا كان بَدّي آكُل
3)	mberiH chefet kalb beneh	مبارح شِفت كَلب بنّي
4)	Henneh chefo Hakim bel beit	هِنّي شافوا حَكيم بالبَيت
5)	ento kein badkoun tchoufo el mouHameh	إنتو كان بَدكُن تشوفوا المُحامي

EXERCISE NUMBER 4

Translate:

1.   Summer starts in June, winter starts in December, and fall starts in September.

_____

_____

2.   I saw the doctor in July and I had a meeting with Jad in February.

_____

_____

3.   In August, I want to go to the beach because the sun is very strong and it's very hot.

_____

_____

4.   We go to the beach in July.

_____

5.   My house will be fixed in March.

_____

6.   Monday, Chadi had a meeting with the architect. He wanted to fix his apartment that is at the end of the street in a white short building. The architect told him that the project requires one month.

_____

_____

_____

7.   I have school every Monday, Tuesday, and Friday.

_____

_____

8.   The teacher gave me good grades on Friday and on Saturday I had a party.

_____

_____

Answers:

1)   El sayf byeje bi Hzayran, el cheteh byeje bi kenoun el awwal wel kharif byeje bi 2ayloul.

الصَيف بيجي بِحزَيران، الشتي بيجي بكانون الأوّل والخَريف بيجي بأيلول

2)   Chefet el Hakeem bi tammouz w ken 3ende maw3ad ma3 Jad bi chbat.

شفت الحَكيم بتَمّوز وكان عَندي مَوعَد مَع جاد بشباط

3)   Bi 2eib, bade rouH 3al ba7er li2ano el chames ktir awwiyeh w ktir chob.

بأب، بَدّي روح على بَحر لأنّو الشَمس كتير قَويّة كتير شوب

4)   Men rouH 3al baHer bi tammouz.

مِنروح على بَحر بتَمّوز

5)   beyteh raH yetzabat bi 2adar.

بَيتي رَح يتظَبَّط بآدار

6)   El tanein, Chadi ken 3endo maw3ad ma3 el mhandis. Ken bado yzabbet che2to yalle bi ekhir el cheri3 bi bineye bayda 2asireh. El mhandis 2allo eno el machrou3 bado chaher waHad.

التّنين، شادي كان عَندو مَوعَد مَع المهَندِس. كان بَدو يظَبِّط شِتتو يَلّي بآخِر الشارع ببنايِة بَيضا قَصيرة. المهَندِس قَلّو إنّو المَشروع بَدو شَهر.

7)   3ende madraseh kel taneyn, taleta w jem3a.

عَندي مَدرَسِة كِلّ تَنَين، تلاتا و جمعَة.

8)   el m3almeh 3atetne 3alemet mnee7a el jem3a wel sabet ken 3ende sahra.

المعلِّمة عَطَتني عَلامات منيحَة الجمعَة والسَبت كان عَندي سَهرَة.

EXERCISE NUMBER 5:

Translate:

M : Hi, How are you today ?

_____

T: I am good. How are you? How is your family?

_____

M: My family is good. My children will be going to school in September.

___

T: How many kids do you have?

___

M: I have 4, two boys and two girls. And you, do you have any kids?

___

T: Yes I have 1. He starts school in October.

___

M: How is your wife? What does she do for a living?

___

T: My wife is good. She is an employee and she will have her own supermarket soon.

___

___

M: Wow! Will she have everything?

___

T: Yes, cheese, butter, jam, cucumbers, green beans, green peas, tomatoes, beetroots, apples, oranges, cherries, strawberries.... Almost everything!

___

___

Answer:
M: marHaba, kifak el yom?
T: mniH. enta kif? kif 3ayltak?
M: 3aylteh mniHa. wleideh raH ykouno rayHin 3al madrase bi ayloul.
T: kam walad 3andak?
M: 3andeh arb3a. sabyein w beintein. w enta 3andak wleid?
T: eh 3ande waHad. bi ballich madrase bi tecrhin el awwal.
M: kifa martak? chou btechtegil?
T: marteh mniHa. hiyyeh mwazaffeh w raH ysir 3anda supermarket la ela ariban.
M: waw! raH ykoun 3anda kel chi?
T: eh, jebne, zebdeh, mrabba, khyar, fasolya khadra, foul akhdar, banadoura, chmandar, teffeH, laymoun, karaz, fraise... ta2riban kel chi!

م: مَرحَبا، كيفْك اليوم؟

ت: منيح. إنتَ كيف؟ كيف عَيلتَك؟

م: عَيلتي منيحة. ولادي رَح يكونو رايحين على مَدرَسة بأيلول

ت: كَم وَلَد عَندَك؟

م: عَندي أربعة. صَبيين و بنتين. و إنتَ عَندَك ولاد؟

ت: إي عَندي وَلَد. بِبَلِّش مَدرَسة بتشرين الأوَّل

م: كيفا مَرتَك؟ شو بتشتغِل؟

ت: مَرتي منيحة. هيّ موَظَّفة و رَح يصير عَندا سوبر ماركت لإلا قَريباً

م: واو! رَح يكون عَندا كِلّ شي؟

ت: إي، جِبنة/ زبدة، مرَبّة، خيار، فصوليا خضرا، فول أخضَر، بَندورَة، شمَندَر، تفّاح، لّيمون، كرَز، فريز... تَقريباً كِلّ شي

CHAPTER 11: EXTRA

In this extra chapter, I will go in-depth into conjugating a verb in order to explain all the confusion that my students usually encounter.

Verb to watch: Hodir
(In order to know the root of the verb, you should put it in the masculine third person singular , in the past simple tense: houwweh Hodir)

PRESENT TENSE

The present simple indicates a general state:

I watch television every night: ana boHdar television kell leileh (present simple verbs always start with a "b" except when preceded by the we pronoun: we watch neHna mnoHdar)

The present continuous is used for an action that is happening now: I am watching a series: ana 3am boHdar mousalsal

Present Simple Tense	Present Continuous
ana boHdar	3am boHdar
enta btoHdar	3am toHdar
enteh btoHdareh	3am toHdareh
houwweh byoHdar	3am yoHdar
hiyye btoHdar	3am toHdar
neHna mnoHdar	3am noHdar
ento btoHdaro	3am toHdaro
henneh byoHdaro	3am yoHdaro

Examples:

We usually watch the game together: 3adatan, neHna mnoHdar el moubarat sawa.

We are watching the game together: 3am noHdar el moubarat sawa.

PAST TENSE

Now that we covered the present tenses, let's move on to the past:

The past simple indicates an action that happened once in the past:
I traveled to Spain last year: ana sefaret 3a espania el seneh el madyeh.

The "used to + infinitive" tense indicates an action that used to take place in the past, but doesn't happen anymore:
I used to eat meat, but now I'm a vegetarian: ana kenet ekoul laHmeh, bas hala' soret nabeitiyeh.

Past simple	"used to + infinitive"
ana Hdoret	kenet oHdar
enta Hdoret	kenet toHdar
ente Hdorteh	kenteh toHdareh
houwe Hodir	ken yoHdar
hiyye Hodrit	kenit toHdar
neHna Hdorna	kenna noHdar
ento Hdorto	kento toHdaro
henneh Hodro	keno yoHdaro

Examples:

Last year, they watched the game together: el seneh el madyeh, Hodro el moubarat sawa.

Every year, they used to watch the game together: kell sene, keno yoHdaro el moubarat sawa.

FUTURE TENSE

The future tense, probably the easiest, indicates an action that will happen in the future. You only need to remove the "b" from the present simple, and add "raH" before the verb:

I will watch a performance tomorrow: ana raH oHdar 3ared bukra.

Future Tense
ana raH oHdar
enta raH toHdar
enteh raH toHdareh
houwweh raH yoHdar
hiyyeh raH toHdar
neHna raH noHdar
ento raH toHdaro
henneh raH yoHdaro

Examples:

What will you watch tomorrow: shou raH toHdar bokra?

The war will end soon: el Hareb raH tokhlas areeban.

STATE VERBS

There's also the state verbs (as I call them). They are the kind of verbs that are generally used to determine a state like hungry, thirsty, tired, busy. They are all conjugated the same:

shou Hadir min afleim Scorsese?: Which Scorsese movies have you seen?

They also indicate an action:

They run after fame: henneh rekdeen wara el chohra

Pronouns	State Verb
ana/enta/houwweh	Hadir
ana/enteh/hiyyeh	Hadra
neHna/ento/henneh	Hadreen

More examples of state verbs:

We are hungry, do you have anything to eat? : neHna jou3anin, 3andkoun chi lal akeil?

She is very busy, she cannot reply to the phone: hiyyeh ktir machgouleh, ma fiya tred 3al telephone

95

I am going to the market in the afternoon, does anyone need something?:ana rayiH 3al sou2 ba3ed el doher, Hadan baddo chi?

The old woman is very tired, we should take her to the hospital: el mara el kbeereh/khotyara kteer te3beneh, lezim nekheda 3al mestachfa

Who is going to the concert tomorrow night? : min rayiH 3al concert/ Hafleh el mousi2iyyeh boukra 3achiyyeh?

Who is coming with me to Tripoli? : min jeyeh ma3e 3a Trablous?

VERB TO SEE

Now that we have gone through these tenses, let's apply them by conjugating the verb "to see".

I see : ana bchouf/ 3am chouf / cheyfeh

Present simple:
I see the birds flying in September: ana bshouf el 3safir tayreen bi ayloul (tayreen is a state verb here).

Present contious:
I am seeing the birds from my window: ana 3am shouf el 3safeer min shebbeikeh.

State verb:
sheyif el baHer shou kbeer: Do you see how big the sea is? (from the famous Feyrouz song)

Past simple:
Who saw me in the interview?: meen sheifneh bil mou2abaleh?

Past continuous:
They used to see their father every day: henneh keino yshoufo bayyoun kell yom.

Future:
I will see your mom in Dubai and I will tell her hi from your side: raH shouf emmik bi dubai w sallemlik 3leya.

TIPS

Verbs and pronouns:

Another topic that always intrigues my students is that of the "indirect objects": how do we say "I saw her" in Lebanese? "I dreamt of you"? "I will tell them"? …
The answer is very easy! You simply add the pronoun you need to the verb, sometimes with little adjustments to make the verb sounds lighter…

For the third person, we add an "o" at the end if it's a masculine pronoun, and an "a" if it's feminine, and "oun" if it's plural:

I saw	shefet
I saw him	shefto
I saw her	shefta
I saw them	sheftoun

Tip: The "e" that is dropped from the end of "shefet" is only a matter of dialect. In some regions, you could say "sheft" instead of "shefet".

For the second person, we add "ak" if it's masculine, "ik" if it's feminine, and "koun" if it's plural:

I dreamt	Hlemet
I dreamt of you (masculine)	Hlemtak
I dreamt of you (feminine)	Hlemtik
I dreamt of you (plural)	Hlemtkoun

Examples:

I will write you a letter: raH ekteblik maktoub

I will travel with her to see you : rah sefir ma3a ta choufkoun

I will send you a song: rah eb3atlak / waddilak ghenniyeh

Sing us a song: ghannilna ghenniyeh

Can you get me water: fik tjebleh may?

Tell me your name: 2elleh chou esmak

Can you tell him how to go to hamra: fikeh tfasrilo kif birouH 3al hamra?

Will you show her her room? : btfarjiya oudeta?

CONCLUSION

If you enjoyed the book, I would be very glad if you leave an honest review on the Amazon page of the book. The reviews will help me know what works and what doesn't, so I can fix that in this book, as well as in subsequent volumes. To leave a review, please go to the Amazon page, scroll down to the end of the reviews, and click on "Write a customer review".

The book's Amazon page could be accessed here:
https://lebanese-arabic.com/Vol2

Thank you for reading my book, I hope you found it to be helpful. In case you have any questions about the Lebanese Dialect, feel free to post it on either my Facebook page, or as a comment on my videos:

FACEBOOK PAGE:

Learn Lebanese Arabic
http://bit.ly/LearnLebaneseArabicFB

YOUTUBE CHANNEL:

hiibanajem
http://bit.ly/hiibanajem1

And finally, if you would like to be notified of new videos, lessons and books please enter your email address here:
http://bit.ly/FBolVIDoptin
or send me an email on:
lebaneselessons@gmail.com

ABOUT THE AUTHOR

Hiba Najem, has been teaching Lebanese Arabic online since 2011, and has enhanced her method according to her students' needs and feedback. The social aspect of online teaching has helped her in developing her teaching into a very effective style.

Made in the USA
Columbia, SC
15 October 2024

44408585R00063